Understanding Before Undertaking

With Other Lovely Stories

By

Jessica Stevenson

Table of contents

Introduction

"Dear, I'm so worn out. I'm losing, I can't handle this. Gabriel saw his wife on her knees in excruciating prayer when he entered his bedroom to continue venting. She continued to pray despite his attempts to capture her attention. Gabriel entered the two-seater, looking worn out and desolate. The weary look on his face suggests a lot is going on in his life and at home. Despite his best efforts, nothing seemed to be working. Even though he was having financial difficulties, his kids continued to fall unwell every month. He frequently questioned whether he was still a child of God or whether God was simply ignoring him.

Gabriel has been going through a financial downturn despite being a hard-working and devoted Christian. As the family's sole provider, his meager income was insignificant. Three weeks is hardly enough time for it. The situation will only become worse when each month ends and the pay is paid because one by one, his children will start to get sick. The salary will therefore be used at the hospital. Of course, he had to put their well-being first. They frequently had nothing or very little to deal with for the remainder of the month.

I know the Lord is on my side to see me through..

The story continues

Chapter 1

Our Dependable captain

The definitions of Lord and Captain are similar in the dictionary. Lord refers to a person who possesses strength, influence, or authority; other synonyms include leader, monarch, and commander. The term "captain" refers to a commander, head of a group, or person in charge—chief, leader, or ship's commander.

When we accept Jesus into our lives and hold fast to His teachings, we give Him the authority and title of

"Lord and Captain" over our lives. He wants to have a relationship with every one of us so that we will follow and trust Him wholeheartedly. He joins us on the journey through life to guide us down the best path He has prepared for us.

Your confidence and hope will be certain and secure thanks to the Anchor Truth you have placed in your heart. Jesus is the captain of your life when he is present. He delivers instructions, assumes leadership, is familiar with marine hazards, and can guide you through, over, and even around them.

The Master and His Disciples were meant to board another boat and travel to a different city, but it ended up being a turning point in their lives. The Master decided to take a nap as the boat smoothly crossed the river, and the Disciples chose to simply soak in the peace of the open sea. Then, out of nowhere, a fierce storm erupted that threatened to engulf the boot and all inside.

The Disciples panicked as they should have because this was too much for them. They screamed out, "Master, do you not care that we perish? The Master rose with His customary composure, chastised the winds and the waves, and commanded, "Peace, be silent." Surprisingly, the storm complied! What kind of man is this, that even the wind and the sea follow him? everyone who saw this magnificent miracle wondered in awe. (Mark 4:35-41).

You don't need to speculate too much about who He is because the Bible already tells us specifics about Him. He is our trustworthy Captain; the one with the capacity to guide you through life's journey and lead you to the successful outcome of your circumstances. He is the only one who has the power to command the winds of adversity, servitude, and anguish in your life to cease. He is Jesus, the Son of the Alive God and the World's Savior.

"The LORD powerful and great, the LORD mighty in war," describes him

(Psalm 24:8). He has the power to end every conflict you are currently experiencing. He is unmatched; in fact, he is a powerful warrior and the refuge from the storms of life. He is not only powerful but also charming. He wants to be your buddy who is closer than a brother, not merely the captain of the boat of your life (Proverbs 18:24).

We need this trustworthy Captain to be at the helm of our life's boat now more than ever because the world is becoming more unpredictable, turbulent, and harsh. It is only prudent to seek refuge in the bosom of the One who is the Giver of life and who is aware of life's measurements. He is the Truth, the

Life, and the Way. What more could a person want? Declare your allegiance to this Captain if you haven't already, and you'll be doing yourself a big favor. Only He can guide you through life's ups and downs. He is the only Anchor who is firm, safe, and certain. You may count on Him because He is the dependable CAPTAIN.

Recognize the offering He made on the Cross of Calvary in your place. Admit your sins and make amends. Ask Him to come into your life as your Lord and Savior, and beg for His pardon. Continue to develop your relationship with Him; it doesn't end there. By reading, reflecting on, and memorizing His Word, spend time

listening to Him. One of the most important defenses you can put on to endure the rough seas of life is your commitment to living your life by His will. Trust Him completely, and allow Him to take up your cause in warfare.
There are only two sides to conflicts in life: the winning side and the losers' lane. The trusty and unbeatable Captain Jesus is on the winning team. Align yourself with Him today, and let Him handle the rest.
When Jesus is at the helm, your life likewise has a course.
Without Him, our lives would be like ships at sea, drifting aimlessly without a compass or map. Without direction or purpose, we shall merely float. We have to be ready to go

where He leads. While we may not always know our final destination, He does, and that is sufficient. With Jesus as our Lord and Captain, we are in the best hands possible. Each of us is about to embark on a magnificent journey, and He assures us that He will be there every step of the way.

Chapter 2

Educating yourself before acting

Under a guava tree, Beauty and Linda sat in awkward quiet, both of them waiting for the other to speak first. Beauty waited eagerly and questioned why Linda was silently sitting there. She occasionally moved her seat, and when the stillness became intolerable, she yelled, "Look, Linda, I know you are here to question me why I haven't been coming to the church."

Lindo answered, "I'm sorry if I offended you; I was simply wondering how to start this dialogue without appearing critical or offensive.

I understand, Beauty murmured after pausing for a while.
"I hope you're doing well," Lino enquired. Beauty sadly shook her head in response and said, "No, I'm not fine. Due to my perception that attending church is worthless, I have stopped going. Yes, it's futile, she said, observing Lindo's reaction. First, my husband passed away, leaving me to care for four kids by myself. My third child is critically ill, my first son is being kept in police custody for a crime he did not commit, my pay is not exactly stellar, and I recently found a growth on my chest. I have prayed in a variety of ways and gone to a variety of places of worship, yet I am still at the same

place. You know, I originally considered waiting for death to arrive, but I'm not sure I can wait any longer. I might end it and put an end to this wretched life.

"Beauty!" You can't talk like that, Linda yelled. Your life is not yours to take; you cannot do so. Are you truly giving up on God, Beauty?

"You have no idea how it would feel to be in my position right now. You have no concept of what it is like to beg God for help, and instead of receiving answers, you are only receiving additional issues. If there is a God, he has abandoned me there is, Beauty sadly said.

"Beauty, God hasn't forgotten about you. Even though your position may appear to be beyond hopeless, He is with you right now, working things out for your benefit. Listen, He might have had a reason for allowing every event in your life. Even though you may not realize it now, as you progress through this life, you will know why you had to go through this. Also, keep in mind that He promised not to let you experience anything above your capabilities. Beauty, you are more resilient than you realize. God is still in control of your life because He loves you. Get over this despair and depression, and turn to God once more. He won't let you down. Linda gave her support.

"Hmm!" Gorgeous sighed.

"Hear me, see. All of these could simply be the devil's strategy to make God look bad so that you lose confidence in Him. We both agree that God is absolutely real, powerful, and capable of going above and beyond everything we could ask or imagine. Come back to God, Beauty, and let's place new faith in Him.

Beauty gave her permission, and Linda gently guided her through a time of prayer. In the end, Beauty sensed a glimmer of hope in her heart. And God handled all of her difficulties.

You might not be aware of it, but we are currently engaged in a conflict. This war between light and darkness—this battle for men's souls—has been raging since the Fall of man and is growing more intense as this era draws to a close, causing the human race to suffer senseless suffering. To solve problems or defend themselves, individuals are prepared to do everything, even sell their souls to the devil.

There is no place for standing on the fence or the sidelines as this battle continues. Take a stand-light or go into the dark. Additionally, you need a solid grasp of the tactical guidelines and strategic tenets to prevail in the war of life.

Knowing Life's Struggles

In this realm, there are numerous types of combat. The first is the universal difficulties that every person on earth will experience in life. challenges of human existence; regardless of age, religion, background, financial situation, educational credentials, or race, every mortal will have a fair share. It could take several health forms. obstacles, addictions, financial hardship, postponement of pregnancy or marriage, spiritual issues, unemployment, fear, and various forms of bad luck. Even Christians are susceptible to these difficulties. Christians are distinguished from non-Christians by their assurance and awareness that God has triumphed over the earth and all its difficulties.

The fight to win the human soul has reached a new level. Any of the aforementioned difficulties would be used by the devil to tempt people into turning to him for help, keeping them captive. Additionally, when someone gives their life to the Lord, they are seen as an enemy. To put it another way, the instant you commit your life to Christ, a line is drawn between you and the kingdom of evil, and you are now a target. Since this is war, you cannot live your life as if it were a playground.

Particularly in this time of injury, the Body of Christ is not spared. The Church stands for God's earthly presence, and it is through Her that He will draw souls to Himself. The battle against the Church has taken on a variety of forms, including legal battles, political assassinations, rewritten Scripture, and campaigns to have Jesus' name eliminated from Gospel songs and movies. What about the invasion of the Church by false prophets and brethren who seek to corrupt the Church and carry out crimes in its name, so profane the name of God and discouraging believers and would-be believers? The devil is working tirelessly to drag as many people as he can from the path of grace and into eternal perdition.

Even though it is a biblical reality that all conflicts in life will persist as long as the earth exists, you shouldn't throw in the towel and let the devil wreak havoc in your life. You should get up right now and go after him. Nevertheless, your ability to win any conflict depends on how well you comprehend it.

There are many Christians who think that the devil is the source of all of life's difficulties, but that is untrue. Although many difficulties arise in your life to teach you valuable lessons, force you to make necessary changes, make room for your advancement, the glory of God, and many other things, many difficulties have their origins in Satan, just like the woman Jesus claimed was bound by the devil for many years, the vicissitudes of Job, and others in the

Bible. Therefore, before taking action to find a remedy, you must exercise due diligence to comprehend the nature, cause, or rationale of your current problem.

You can use the best strategy and weapon to fight the war if you have a good understanding of it. Before you start searching for a solution, you should first spend some time to accurately diagnose the problem. Since you won't be trying to fit a round peg into a square hole, the answer will be nearly instantaneous once you have a thorough understanding of the issue.

It will need prayer, Bible study, sensitivity to the Holy Spirit, and a lack of emotion and impatience to understand the issue. Additionally, avoid overly spiritualizing situations and learn about the conflict so you can properly attack it.

Taking the Battle and Winning It

The second step is to take an offensive stance to engage in the war after fully comprehending the conflict you and the Church are facing. How do you engage these wars so that you can win?

One: Invite Jesus in. Many Christians perish in the sea of life's difficulties because they neglect to include Jesus in their conflicts. They believe God already knows and is actively engaged in their conflicts. They don't have it entirely incorrect, but they tend to forget that Jesus is never an intrusion. He is aware of all your problems, but He still requests your invitation. Whether you comprehend the issue or not, the first thing you should do in a difficult circumstance is to invite Jesus into it; avoid the bad habit of calling or going to mortals first. Before you capture folks' attention, a lot can happen. Jesus is the ever-present comforter for those who are in need (Psalm 46: 1).

Two: prepare for the fight. This requires consistently possessing a warrior mentality. That is, using your mind to push back against forces both inside and outside of you that could render you helpless or weak during the actual battle. These forces could be fear, discouragement, concern, self-pity, disappointment, feeling alone in the fight, and more. There must be cast aside to make room for a warrior's mentality that views obstacles as a part of life's constants that must be fought and overcome. Additionally, being prepared for a fight entails keeping an eye out for Na Conic Invasion, having the willpower to overcome any obstacles, and having faith in your Capital. Self-defense, self-affirmation, displaying courage, etc.

Third: Put on the full armor of God. Your battledress, which protects you from head to toe while bottling, is made up of the entire armor of God. It makes you fearsome and provides you with all-around defense, fortitude, courage, hope, and peace. Given that we are constantly at war, we must always wear the full armor of God. No believer ever engages in or prevails in a conflict without wearing protective gear. These shields include the things mentioned in Ephesians 6 as well as righteousness, faith, and the Bible.

Four: Pay attention to others who have overcome comparable obstacles and come out on top. Similar difficulties like those you are experiencing have been encountered, suffered, battled for, and overcome by many Christians. Ask, listen to, and study how they competed and won, then put that knowledge into practice.

You can read books written by modern Christians who conquered odd obstacles despite them.

Five: Imagine the future while showing God some patience. Your struggle will undoubtedly end at some point.

So, wait entirely on God and exercise patience with Him. Don't follow those who wish to overcome their obstacles by any means necessary and at any cost. Furthermore, all wars are about to come to an end. Jesus will shortly return, making all conflicts irrelevant. Consider what these difficulties will be like when Christ arrives and you are caught up in the Rapture as you go through this difficult time. This will enable you to endure hardship patiently while trusting in God and anticipating a successful outcome. Finally, for the resurrection of genuine worship and righteous people to reemerge, the Church needs to clean up every issue through repentance, return to the Scripture, humble Herself, and sincerely pray. To face the enemy, we must rise as a single, holy, and powerful force, and by the power of the Holy Spirit, we will triumph in every conflict. Because Jesus our Captain declares in Matthew 16:18, "I will establish my church upon the rock, and the gates of hell shall not prevail against it".

Chapter 3

Occupy Your Space

"Dear, I'm so worn out. I'm losing, I can't handle this. Gabriel saw his wife on her knees in excruciating prayer when he entered his bedroom to continue venting. She continued to pray despite his attempts to capture her attention. Gabriel entered the two-seater, looking worn out and desolate. The weary look on his face suggests a lot is going on in his life and at home. Despite his best efforts, nothing seemed to be working. Even though he was having financial difficulties, his kids continued to fall unwell every month. He frequently questioned whether he was still a child of God or whether God was simply ignoring him.

Gabriel has been going through a financial downturn despite being a hard-working and devoted Christian. As the family's sole provider, his meager income was insignificant. Three weeks is hardly enough time for it. The situation will only become worse when each month ends and the pay is paid because one by one, his children will start to get sick. The salary will therefore be used at the hospital. Of course, he had to put their well-being first. They frequently had nothing or very little to deal with for the remainder of the month.

Unexpectedly, this started to happen frequently, with the family spending the majority of their meager monthly income on the children's medical expenses. Soon, he started borrowing. Occasionally, he would borrow half of his net income before the month was over. He quickly racked up so much debt that only a miracle could help him pay it off because his salary didn't rise. Ophelia and Michael, however, experienced illnesses every month, and they didn't recover until they had been a few nights in a hospital. Since the children's diseases weren't life-threatening, he never saw the devil's hand at work in the whole situation.

So, on this momentous day, Gabriel nearly lost it when he received the customary call from the school administration informing him that his children had been unwell. They said that they had to phone him because they couldn't reach his wife. He hurried to the school to pick up the kids, then left the office and drove home. When he got home, all he wanted to do was complain and vent to his wife, but instead, he discovered her writhing in agony as she prayed. He attempted to stop her, but she was unresponsive (Shortly before then, she had received a prompting in her spirit to pray for her children that the de- was at it again). Gabriel also wanted to borrow some money from his wife so that he could take the kids to the hospital because he had used the little money he had on them to get them home. He was forced to join her in her prayer because she continued to say nothing.

Infuriated, Valentina and Gabriel turned their attention away from the kids that day and started a one-week prayer and fasting period. They prayed while aware that they were God's children and that Jesus had traded His wealth for their poverty. He had also given them the ability to crush their foes, and by the scars, He bore, they had been made whole. Since the beginning of the family life, they had never prayed thus much, and something did happen. Without being taken to the hospital, the children fully recovered after two days, and that occurrence signaled the end of their seasonal illness. More so, a month later, Gabriel was hired for a higher-paying position that also included a house, a car, health insurance, and money for the kids' schooling, to name a few perks.

There is a lot in the world that has the power to completely undermine one's faith, dear reader. You must constantly remind yourself of who you are in Christ Jesus and how, according to Ephesians 2:6–9, you have been exalted to occupy a place of honor and authority beside Him in the heavenly realms. Going about with a victim's mentality won't be helpful to you or anyone else. The Lord wants you to rule and dominate your environment, leaving no opportunity for the adversary to intervene.

Knowing Your Position in Christ

As a follower of Christ, you must comprehend who you are in Him and the position you hold as a result of Him. You should pray, as Paul did in Ephesians chapter 1, that God will provide you the spirit of wisdom and a revelation of who He is. You should also pray that God will open your eyes to the hope of your calling, the richness of your magnificent inheritance, and the immeasurable power He is at work in you (Ephesians 1:17-19). You won't act like an empty wimp who can be played with or pushed around when

God reveals to you and helps you realize His immense power and greatness and that you, His child, are His living tabernacle. This is because your relationship with Christ places you in a position of power and authority.

According to preceptaustin.org, "Christians are eternally united and connected with Christ because they have a solemn, binding, and irrevocable commitment with Him. When he died, we died. When he was buried, we were buried. When he rose, we were raised. When he was seated at the right hand of His father, we were seated at the right hand of our Father in heaven;" far above all principalities, and powers, and might, and dominion, and every name that is named, not only in this world but also in that which is to come (Ephesians 1:21-23). God expects us to exercise total control over every aspect of our lives, just like our Master does. Because followers of Christ have been raised with Him to sit in heavenly places, God wants us to accomplish the same things that Jesus did, like heal the sick, cast out demons, calm the storm, walk on water, preach hope, and offer a new life. Scripture calls us more than conquerors because of this. By definition, conquerors are champions or victorious in life's conflicts. Every child of God ought to fit the bill here.

What do we become if Jesus is the King of kings? He governs over and alongside believers as kings. According to Revelation 1:6, when we follow him wholeheartedly, we are transformed into priests and kings who rule and shine over their domains. Decide to conquer your planet.

Making Your Space Clear

You need to identify and focus on the God-ordained realm or place where you are called to assume leadership as you come to terms with who you are in Christ and the immense power at your disposal. Christians who are unaware of or underrepresented in their environment will unnecessarily suffer. Own your space and be aware of who you are. Your spiritual space should be your primary priority as a Christian. As soon as you turn from your sins and give Christ control of your life, you are granted access to this area. As you accomplish this, He grants you a place in the "heavenly realms in Christ Jesus" that is spiritual (Ephesians 2:6).

In addition, there is your actual space. This includes, among other things, your spaces as a spouse, parent, worker, or employer, part of the Body of Christ, and your spaces for finances, security, and health. This information enables you to identify your numerous spheres of influence and motivates you to keep a close eye on them so the devil doesn't set up camp there. Knowing your boundaries as a couple means staying inside the boundaries of your marriage and preventing any sort of pollution that could endanger it. This will need you to keep a vigilant eye out for both material and spiritual intruders in your marriage.

Additionally, you must control your emotional environment. If the devil wants to win over a person, he will start with their minds, filling them with dread, worry, anxiety, and other forms of negativity. You are responsible for bringing under control and into the obedience of Christ Jesus every thought that exalts itself against the knowledge of Christ.

You have a significant impact on your children's spiritual, academic, mental, social, and physical well-being as their parents. The enemy will take up the space that was formerly yours in their lives if you are ignorant of this obligation, treat it carelessly, or handle it helplessly. They will also raise a lot of issues for you. Get your grit on and set a positive example for your children by being their spiritual protector, greatest friend, and supporter. The devil's plans to govern and destroy their lives will so be foiled.

The same truth holds to your position in society, whether you are an employer of labor or an employee. You should be aware of your obligations and rights. This will enable you to carry out your duties without being intimidated and to uphold your integrity despite the wicked tactics that permeate every industry. You can also occupy a chaste woman's space in the church. Set a good example for other church ladies by acting righteously, submitting, lovingly, godly, and in service. In reality, being aware of the many spaces you inhabit will enable you to take responsibility for those spaces and serve the Lord in the capacity He desires.

Take the Lead!

It is well known that the devil, our enemy, prowls the world in search of prey. However, those who are outside of God's protection and those who, although being under His protection, have given up their areas for the devil to possess and function in is his rightful prey. Simply put, occupying your area is taking control of the locations that God has designated as your territory. He wants you to be a that strong person who neither the devil nor his minions can enter their spaces or damage their things. How do you establish control or claim your territory?

First, be aware of any potential threats to your space. Sin is the biggest danger to your personal space. Truth be told, sin poses the biggest harm to man since it allows the devil access to one's life, contrary to popular belief, which holds that the devil is the greatest danger to mankind. Because sin is Satan's "Identification Number," he pursues it wherever he finds it, even if there is just the slightest compromise. And when he arrives, he inflicts that life and family with a variety of criticisms and conflicts. God's Word says that "Righteousness exalteth a nation: but sin is a reproach to any people" (Proverbs 14:34).

Two, do the needful. As you discover any potential threat, do both spiritual and physical weeding. Repent from all sins, and do away with every form of sin. If it is requisite knowledge or wisdom you lack, ask God "That giveth to all men liberally, and upbraideth not; and it shall be given [you]" (James 1:5). Three, stand on God's Word. You must be a man or woman of the Word to take absolute charge of your space; you must stand unshakably on the Scripture. Knowing, following, and living by the Word are necessary for standing on His Word. His Word will be effective against the devil's tricks in this way.

Four, contend for God's promises while on your knees. Christian fights are primarily fought invisibly. We battle forces that function in the spiritual world and are invisible to the human eye. The reason Ephesians 6:12 states that "We struggle not against flesh and blood, but against principalities, against powers, against the rulers of the darkness of this age, against spiritual wickedness in high places," is because these are not the enemies we face in this life. As a result, you must battle if you believe the enemy has unnoticed hands in any part of your territory. Through the name of Jesus—the scepter of power and strength—this kind of battle is conducted. As a Christian, you cannot function without prayer; otherwise, the enemy would sabotage your efforts and fully take over your domain. The Bible exhorts you to "Pray without ceasing" (1 Thessalonians 5:17). To put it another way, pray constantly, wherever, and for anything. The God who commands us to pray will undoubtedly be present to hear and respond to our petitions.

Five: Keep an eye out. It is perilous to pray without also watching, which is why the Lord tells us to "Watch and pray" (Matthew 26:41). Being watchful is a crucial aspect of controlling your environment. You should keep a continuous eye out for threats to your region. It will be necessary to do this while being guided by the Holy Spirit. He develops your awareness of what is going on around you, aids in your understanding and discernment of the situation, and inspires you to fight honorably.

Sixth, claim your territory. Never let someone else dominate your environment; always take control of it. Reject sloth, self-indulgence, a lack of prayer, a lack of Bible study, a lack of sensitivity to the voice of the Spirit, and thoughtless behavior. living an unholy lifestyle, making compromises, quitting your job as a servant of God, and similar things. God Almighty Himself will reserve your space as you proceed in the name of Jesus.

Chapter 4

ALL KINDS OF PRAYER

Paul was a prayerful person. Apart from the Lord Jesus Himself, he is the only man who is most suited to teach us the holy art of praying since prayer was the key to his life, his great influence, his endurance and suffering, and his passionate love for men's souls. There are seven essential truths about prayer in the texts that come before us.

1. The Great Essential is prayer

After discussing the armor we should put on, Paul immediately continues, "Praying at all times." A soldier needs to wear the proper armor and have a sword, but it is also crucial that the soldier maintain continual contact with his Commander-in-Chief (Hebrews 2: 10). The prayer line of connection with our risen Lord must never be cut off since the Christian is in direct contact with the throne of God when he is fighting on the battlefield. The greatest necessary is prayer; it is both fundamental and not at all optional.

2. We should always pray.

This reminds us of 1 Thessalonians 5:17, which says that we are to try to live in the same environment and attitude of prayer. Paul not only exhorts us to pray, but to pray "under all circumstances." We must establish regular prayer times, just as Daniel prayed three times daily (Daniel 6:10), David prayed three times daily (Psalm 55:17) and subsequently revealed that he prayed seven times daily (Psalm 119:164), and the Savior, who frequently withdrew into a place of prayer (Luke 6: 12). Then, we can pray at particular times, such as when we're in trouble (Psalm 55: 16), when we need guidance (James 1: 5), when we're being tested, when we're being persecuted, when we're being tempted, when we're being persecuted, when we're being threatened with sickness, when we're threatened with any kind of need, etc (Philippians 4: 6).

3. We need to pray in many different ways.

Prayers can be expressed through adoration, praise, thanksgiving, petition, supplication, or intercession, as indicated by the phrase "all types of prayers and requests." But take into account the three different "kinds" of prayer that are described in Matthew 6:6, the prayer of agreement in Matthew 18:19, and collective prayer (Acts 12: 5).

4. We must continue to pray.

5. All Saints Need Our Prayers.

Although it is impossible to pray specifically for every saint, we can do it in a general and most definitely organized way. For instance, we could consistently and methodically pray for God's suffering saints and God's sinful saints. Ever say a prayer for these? - for backsliders who have been caught up in the tricks of the enemy, for Christians who are tempted and defeated by the world, the body, and the Devil? (3) The confined saints of God. A lot of people who love the Lord are put to one side by illness, which has been allowed to advance the gospel (Philippians 1: 12). These suffering people require prayer so that they may be given the ability to proclaim Christ's sufficiency and power. Pray for new converts (Acts 9:17), workers to be sent forth (Matthew 9:38),

Christian literature to be printed (Psalm 43:3), open doors for the gospel (1 Corinthians 16:9), and the breaking of Satan's power (Luke 13:12–16).

6. We Need to Pray for Those Fighting at the Front Line.

According to verses 19 and 20, persons who hold significant positions in Christian ministry are especially in need of the prayers of God's people; for more information, see Acts 4:29. In God's harvest field, how should we pray for preachers, evangelists, instructors, and leaders? that they might be able to preach the gospel with clarity, courage, and grace.

One "free ride" to God's mystical assistance in prayer. Without this divine assistance, we are unable to endure the fierce struggles of life or lead the magnificent lives God has planned for us. John Piper once remarked "Christ-exalting characteristics that set Christians apart from the world are the result of God's extraordinary grace. And prayer is how God has decided that this gift comes to us. Because of this, prayer must play a fundamental role in our lives, those of our families, and our missions."

Prayer is a potent spiritual weapon that defeats the adversary and gives you the victory you need when used in conjunction with other spiritual weapons supplied by the Bible. One of the greatest blessings of the redeemed is a gift from God to man.

It drives the adversary from the field, causes God to intervene to alter the circumstances, and aids you in winning every conflict.

There are many different methods to pray to God; they don't all have to go in the same direction. You can pray in a variety of ways, including worship and adoration, requests, armed conflict, and intercession. You can acknowledge God's work in your life and thank Him for all He has done for you through prayers of thanksgiving. You can express your worship to God in song, eulogy, or simply by telling

Him how much you admire Him and appreciate everything He has done or is doing for you.

You can offer God your wishes or heart desires in addition to the prayer of thankfulness and trust Him to grant them. According to Philippians 4:6, "Never worry about anything, but instead, cover everything in prayer and supplication. Let God know your petitions in a spirit of appreciation." Talking to God about your issues can help you in two ways: first, it will provide you rest, mental clarity, and relief; and second, it will help you find solutions to your issues. There is another side to bringing problems to Him. Intercessory prayer is the act of bringing other people's concerns to

God so that He can provide them with relief and remedies. As ambassadors of Christ here on earth, we too must do as our Lord Jesus constantly prays for all God's children.

Every Christian must practice the prayer of battle because we are at war all the time with the forces of darkness. You use the Sword of the Spirit, the shield of faith, and every other tool the Bible provides when praying in this way.

Although anyone can pray, only the virtuous' prayers are effective (James 5:16). Therefore, a person must turn from their sins and embrace Jesus as their Lord and Saviour before they may completely benefit from this unique gift. They should also follow

God's laws and heed His commands. God hates sinners' prayers because they are abhorrent to Him. However, when a sinner asks God to forgive them of their sins, He hears them and responds.

There are two ways to pray: privately and publicly, where a larger number of people can contribute to blocking the entrance to Hell. Additionally, a place of prayer may be found anyplace and everywhere. You can pray to a God who is always there. He defies limitations and bounds with his presence. As a result, you shouldn't postpone praying until you are in a quiet area like a church, your home, or a residence. Anywhere and everywhere the Holy Spirit moves you to pray, you can do so. You must pray in the name of JESUS, which is more significant. "Truly, I say to you, Whatever you shall ask the Father in my name, he will give you," he assures you in John 16:23. Your prayers will be heard by God.

Your faith is another essential component of prayer. Without faith, it is impossible to please God because "anyone who comes to God must believe that he is and that he rewards those who earnestly seek him" (Hebrews 11:6). So, while you pray, believe without a shadow of a doubt in your heart, and the Lord will grant your requests in the name of Jesus.

Chapter 5

Strength in the word of the Lord

Everyone may count on us to help them overcome difficulties. Many people rely on relationships, family, fortune, knowledge, and strategies to get through challenging circumstances. But the Bible continues to be the most reliable source of our needed strength. It is reliable because it provides unending comfort, light, assurance, hope, and solace, which converts into superhuman power. This is my comfort in my affliction: for thy word has quickened me, the Psalmist wrote in Psalm 119:50.

Your closest friend amid adversity ought to be God's Word. It should permeate your body and be kept in your mouth, heart, mind, and head so that you can use it when necessary to draw power during trying times. Because God's Word is God Himself, relying on it for support is equivalent to relying on God. "In the beginning was the Word, and the Word was with God, and the Word was God," declares John 1:1.

The Bible also refers to the Bible as the Bread of Life. It satisfies the soul. When the devil attacks your faith and you are about to give up, all it takes to enliven and strengthen your inner man is an injection of God's Word into your soul. I am tormented very much; quicken me, O Lord, according to thy Word, the Psalmist cried to God, realizing this (Psalm 119:107). The Bible also serves as a candle for your feet (Psalm 119:103), illuminating your path through the world's roving darkness. So, to draw strength from the Word, you must first have a personal relationship with God.

Knowing or having God as your Lord is the only requirement for having a connection with God and the Bible. This requires that you fully repent of your sins and receive Jesus Christ, who is the Word made flesh, into your life as your Lord and Savior. The Word only begins to make sense to you and in your circumstances once this has been resolved. The reason for this is that as soon as you accepted Jesus as your personal Savior, God pours out His Spirit within you, illuminating your intellect with the Scripture: "For the letter killeth, but the spirit gives life" (2 Corinthians 3:6).

You will also need to read, study, or hear the Word ministered to you every day. These are methods by which as a human, the Word can enter your body. Therefore, be diligent in daily studying the Bible in-depth to create an inner reservoir from which you can draw spiritual energy to meet your needs daily. You can make sure you continue your regular study of God's Word by using a daily devotional book, reading the Bible year-round, or listening to recorded sermons.

Additionally, you must store the Word in the correct areas of your being. Consider the Word in your thoughts. The Word is ingrained in your mind, heart, subconscious mind, and mouth as you meditate on it. By doing this, the Word becomes ingrained in you to the point that it provides you with the strength to endure whatever happens without collapsing. By meditating on the Word, you also make it the closest speech in your mouth, speaking the Word to your circumstance rather than admitting weakness and defeat under hard circumstances.

Believing and applying the Word to your circumstances is an essential part of drawing strength from the Bible. Whatever your circumstances, trusting in the Word is believing in God. If you trust the Bible, you will put it to use in your situations. Knowing that the Bible has a promise for every circumstance that arises in human existence is consoling. Apply them to your situation by speaking that promise into the difficulty as you search for and find them. By doing this, you are merely presenting the Lord with your case and your compelling arguments as instructed in Isaiah 41:21.

The integrity of God is generally upheld by the Word. He will never break His word because He values it more than His name. You will not only find strength in the Word, but you will also find God's miraculous intervention via the Word if you can trust, relax, and depend on it when you are faced with puzzling circumstances.

CHAPTER 6

Hold The Fort

The devil is aware that the time is almost up. The struggle waged by the forces of darkness grows more intense, and the suffering endured by the human race is unbearable. Even Christians are starting to panic as their hearts are starting to weaken. Although nothing appears certain, do not be alarmed; the Lord has vowed to be by your side forever (Matthew 28:20). Every believer should at this time:

(1) FOCUS ON JESUS (Hebrews 12:2). In John 16:33, Christ reveals: "These things have been said to you so that you may have peace in me. You will experience hardship in this world, but have hope—I have overcome the world." You should put your trust in Him and look to Him as

the Author and Finisher of your faith since He has conquered the world and all of its difficulties. Consider Him in terms of the attitude He would have adopted if He had been in your position. Act how Jesus would have acted if He had been the one facing your situation, to put it another way.

(2) STAND on God's Word. Every conundrum that man encounters has an answer in God's Word. Every problem has a scriptural solution that can address it. All you have to do is look for that promise in the Bible and cling to it while you make your case to God. Let the Word, rather than the challenge, fill and rule your head, heart, mind, emotion, and mouth.

Therefore, always confess what the Bible says about your circumstance, and you will undoubtedly prevail.

(3) PRAY without dizziness. It is a reality that the devil steals your motivation to pray during trials to make you feel fearful and helpless. You should resist his tricks by remaining persistently steeped in the spirit of prayer. In difficult times, prayer accomplishes a lot: it trains your mind to ignore the apparent, replenishes your strength, and it gives you the confidence that God will hear you and make the necessary intervention. "Call upon me in the day of tribulation; I will deliver thee," says Psalm 50:15. Every time you are

faced with a hardship, you should take your burdens to the Lord first; it should not be the last resort.

(4) PUT ON YOUR ARMOR OF FAITH. Having faith in God is trusting that He has the power to change your difficult circumstances. Do you recall Hezekiah and the bizarre nature of his death sentence? However, he grabbed the bull by the horns. In faith that God could turn the sentence around, he turned to Him in prayer. God responds to your faith by changing your circumstances because it shows Him how much trust you have in Him.

(5) STAY AT YOUR DUTIES POINT. In difficult times, many believers leave their positions of service. This is extremely risky territory to travel since it will allow the devil access to your life and erode your faith. Don't give up on the Body of Christ, no matter what service you provide. Continue sharing the gospel, praying for others, helping out where you can, etc. When you are in need, God, who sees your dedication, will be there for you.

(6) LEARN the lessons that were intended. Every tricky situation teaches us important things. To learn them, make sure you are contemplative and attentive enough.

Some can simply serve to move you nearer to God, while others might guide you toward your breakthrough. Avoid missing out on this crucial component of overcoming obstacles.

7) Feel GRATEFUL. Many people ponder the justification for expressing gratitude under adverse circumstances. In tough times, there are so many things for which to be thankful. The Bible commands us to do this, first of all, saying, "In everything give thanks: for this is the desire of God in Christ Jesus concerning you" (1 Thessalonians 5:18). In addition, you should give thanks to God that your circumstances are not worse. Thank

God for His Word and sure promises, as well as for the love, care, support, and compassion of others. Thank God that you have hope in Christ. In trying times, there is plenty for which to give thanks to God.

The Lord will give you the required victory as you carry out all of these tasks, in the name of Jesus.

CHAPTER 7

EQUIPPED FOR BATTLE

"Pastor, I have prayed in many different ways, but nothing has helped." Thomas cried out. "I fasted for twenty-one days last month, and I almost passed out. Even still, the dreams persist, and I continue to hear bizarre voices that nobody else can hear."

"My brother, you cannot give up now; you must continue in prayer."

But I'm not getting any results; I'm on the verge of losing my head.

"Brother Thomas, you don't have the luxury of losing this battle. The devil is playing tricks on you. You must stand your ground and defend yourself with all of God's arsenal of weapons. Thomas grilled her.

"Yes. Have you forgotten what Ephesians 6:13–18 says? "Therefore, take the full armor of God with you, that you may be able to endure in the terrible day and, having done all, to stand." Therefore, take up your position while wearing the breastplate of righteousness, the preparation for the gospel of peace, and, most importantly, the shield of faith, with which you will be able to snuff out all the fiery darts of the wicked. And put on the sword of the Spirit, which is the word of God; take the helmet of salvation; and say, "Pray continually with all prayer and supplication in the Spirit; and watch thereunto with all perseverance and supplication for all saints."

"It's possible that you haven't been using the proper tools to fight this conflict. You must go back and properly arm yourself with everything that was mentioned in the Bible reference that was just read to you. God is more than capable of winning this battle."

No matter how intense our conflicts are or who is driving them, being well-equipped all the time is a surefire way to come out on top. So how and what do you arm yourself with is the question.

Imagine a brave and skilled soldier who goes to battle without any weapons or ammunition. In such a war, he will undoubtedly suffer serious injuries, if not deadly. The same is true for a believer who engages in daily combat with fleshly weapons; in the process, they will sustain injuries or even perish. Therefore, you must arm yourself with the entirety of God's armor, or spiritual weapons of war.

The warning from the Bible is found in Ephesians 6:11–13 "Put on the full armor of God so that you can withstand the devil's tricks. Because we do not battle against physical opponents but rather against spiritual ones in high places, against principalities, against powers, and against those who control this world's darkness. Take therefore the full armor of God with you so that you can withstand in the day of evil." So, what exactly are these armors?

(1) BELT OF TRUTH: Ephesians 6:14 instructs, "Therefore stand, having your loins girt about with

truth." Satan wants to enslave you by telling you that you can never defeat sin or be free from it. As a result, you will always live under his rule. However, Jesus asserts that knowing the truth will set you free (John 8:32). If you arm yourself with the truth of God's Word—the truth about His love, forgiveness, salvation, righteousness, power, authority, redemption, freedom from Satan's dominion, eternal life in Christ, and other things—you can be free from Satan's deceptions, intimidations, and assaults. You'll be able to keep all the other armors together with the help of the truth of who God is and the authority of His Word. That is, it makes it possible for you to lead a moral and successful life.

(2) BREASTPLATE OF JUSTICE: The breastplate of righteousness shields and guards your heart against contamination, much as a breastplate protects a soldier's heart and other critical organs on the battlefield (Ephesians 6: 14). The Lord Jesus spoke frequently about the importance of diligently guarding the heart, keeping it pure, and defending it against the desecration and trickery of Satan. Since no one is righteous in and of themselves, God has provided us with Jesus, who grants us His righteousness. God then asks that we always wear the righteousness of

Jesus. Not our righteousness, but He provides us with complete protection from Satan's pollution and defeat. The enemy is kept at bay and rendered untouchable by righteousness. The breastplate of righteousness strengthens us even when the obstinate foe dares to attack: "the righteous are brave as a lion" (Proverbs 28:1).

(3) SHOES OF THE GOSPEL: "And the preparation of the gospel of peace shall gird up your feet" (Ephesians 6:15). Your feet need to be safeguarded during the battle since they are as vital as any other part of your body as soldiers of Christ. Because He wouldn't want your feet

hurt on the battlefield, the Lord has provided the shoes of the Gospel for this. The Lord desires for us to put on these evangelism-related shoes so that we might follow Him wherever He leads us while preaching, winning souls, and building His Kingdom. How lovely upon the heights are the feet of him who brings good news, who publishes peace; who brings good news of good, who publishes salvation; who proclaim to Zion, "Thy God reigns," according to Isaiah 52:7.

We can walk in Christ's footsteps, listen to His voice, and carry out His works by donning the shoes of the Gospel. Additionally, wearing the Gospel shoes will enable you to step over any obstacles the devil may lay in your road, such as snakes and scorpions, without suffering any harm (Luke 10: 19). Additionally, it ensures that the Lord is constantly present with you: "Lo, I am with you always, even to the end of the world" (Matthew 28:20).

(4) SHIELD OF FAITH: Taking the shield of faith, with which you will be able to snuff out all the fiery darts of the wicked, is the first thing Ephesians 6:16 advises. One of the armor pieces the Lord expects His children to have is the shield of faith. During conflicts, a shield is utilized to deflect some attacks like precise arrows and other deadly penetrating

weaponry. It is given to you as one of the armors to assist you in deflecting any darts of uncertainty, fear, discouragement, temptation, and other things hurled at you from the domain of evil.

God gives faith to His children as a gift, but He also expects you to grow it until it is strong enough to block all the enemy throws at you and keep you safe. Putting on the armor of faith means modeling your daily life after that of the Son of God. God can keep you during this heavenly journey and prevent you from slipping into the devil's traps because of your complete dependence on Him.

(5) HELMET OF SALVATION: "And put on the helmet of salvation" (Ephesians 6:17). One of the most crucial components of the human body is the head. A proverb holds that everything ends when the head is cut off. To protect their heads, soldiers wear helmets on the battlefield. In the same way, while they contend with principalities and powers daily, followers of Christ need to shield their heads by donning the helmet of their salvation. Since the head is where human thinking and the mind reside, you must safeguard it by being aware of your salvation from the devil's corrupting infiltration, influence, and deception.

Here, the assurance that you have repented of your sins and have received God's forgiveness through Christ Jesus our Saviour serves as the helmet of salvation. It is proof that you are now living by God's grace after being purified of all sin. It involves making sure you are continuing in the eternal life that God has granted you via His Son, Jesus. Without the helmet of salvation, you cannot fight and triumph in the war of life.

(6) SWORD OF THE SPIRIT: The word of God is the "sword of the Spirit," according to verse six (Ephesians 6:17). Without the Sword of the Spirit, having all of God's

defensive armament is like showing up to battle unprepared. The only offensive tool available to Christians today to combat Satan and his army of evil spirits is the Sword of the Spirit, also known as the Bible or the Word of God. The Bible is more accurate, potent, and razor-sharp than any other writing. When tempted by Satan, Our Lord Jesus utilized this weapon, and He prevailed. You should arm yourself with this potent weapon and employ it at all times if you want to triumph against temptation and all of life's conflicts.

How has the Bible changed your life? To become familiar with its strength and truth, read, research, and meditate on it. As you move forward, follow it, accept it as true, and speak it into every circumstance you encounter. Your eyes will be opened to other offensive weapons, such as the name and blood of Jesus, as a result of reading the Bible, which is another advantage.

7) PETITION: "Praying continually in the Spirit, with all prayer and supplication, and watching thereunto with all perseverance and supplication for all the saints" (Ephesians 6:18). Apostle Paul concluded his advice on the necessity to put on the full armor of God with prayer because he understood how crucial prayer is to be victorious in life. This is so that every component

of the armor can be continuously strengthened through prayer. We are to watch and wait with prayer for ourselves and others. Through prayer, you remain constantly in God's presence and under His watchful care. Both in and out of season, pray.

If you fight with the proper tools, you will unquestionably come out stronger at the end of the war. Therefore, arm yourself with prayer and God's whole arsenal so you can confront whatever battles the devil throws your way on the trip home and win. In the name of Jesus, may the Lord give you success?

www.ingramcontent.com/pod-product-compliance
Lightning Source LLC
LaVergne TN
LVHW050328160826
845677LV00014B/3566

* 9 7 9 8 3 7 0 4 0 5 5 2 5 *